Machu Picchu

M I K A Y A P R E S S

NEW YORK

Author's note

Every book is a journey, and each journey is unique. The voyage to Machu Picchu was remarkably enriched by travelers along the way. Whether the encounters were brief or extended, planned or serendipitous, each expanded my thinking and deepened my understanding of a complex subject. I'm grateful to Dave and Nancy Jones, Peter and Cynthia Rockwell, Lola Salas, Rocio Romero, Professor Manuel Burga, Inkas Empire Tours, Francis Casapino Gonzalez, and Jean-Pierre Protzen.

I acknowledge a special debt to Andean scholar Adriana von Hagen, co-author (with Craig Morris) of The Cities of the Ancient Andes. *She brought to her many critical readings of the manuscript patience, wisdom, experience, and great good humor. Any errors of fact and interpretation are mine alone.*

Books by Elizabeth Mann
The Brooklyn Bridge
The Great Pyramid
The Great Wall
Hoover Dam
The Panama Canal
The Roman Colosseum
Tikal
Empire State Building
The Parthenon
Taj Mahal
Statue of Liberty
Little Man

Editor: Stuart Waldman
Design: Lesley Ehlers Design
Copyright © 2000 Mikaya Press

Library of Congress Cataloging-in-Publication Data

Mann, Elizabeth, 1948-
    Machu Picchu / by Elizabeth Mann ; with illustrations by Amy Crehore.
        p. cm. – (A wonders of the world book)
    Includes index.
    Summary: Describes the history of the Inca civilization and the construction of the city of Machu Picchu in the Andes Mountains.
    ISBN 978-1-931414-10-4
    1. Machu Picchu Site (Peru)–Juvenile literature. 2. Incas–Juvenile literature. [1. Machu Picchu Site (Peru) 2. Incas. 3. Indians of South America.] I. Crehore, Amy, 1953- ill. II. Title. III. Series.

    F3429.1. M3 M39 2000
    985'.37–dc2   99-055172

                        10 9 8 7 6 5

                        Printed in China

Machu Picchu

A WONDERS OF THE WORLD BOOK

BY ELIZABETH MANN

WITH ILLUSTRATIONS BY AMY CREHORE

MIKAYA PRESS

NEW YORK

The rain-wet path was overgrown with moss and trees, and Hiram Bingham stumbled as he tried to keep up with the peasant boy who was leading him higher and higher. The chances of finding any trace of Inka life on this mountain ridge high above the Urubamba River seemed as remote as the place itself. Gasping from the difficult climb and distracted by spectacular views through the drifting fog, he didn't realize at first what he was seeing. Then, like an image appearing as a photograph develops, the shapes came into focus. He could make out buildings and terraces and stairways. Through the tangled plants he glimpsed stone walls that were as finely made as works of art.

Bingham couldn't know on that day in July, 1911, the true significance of the mountain settlement the boy had led him to. Machu Picchu, as it is now called, had been built more than four centuries earlier by the mightiest of all Inka emperors, Pachacuti, at the height of his power. Once it had been a place of great importance, a royal estate and a religious center. Now it was so overgrown with trees, vines, and orchids as to be almost invisible. Incredibly, beneath the dense foliage, the buildings were still much as they had been in 1532 when Spanish explorers invaded the Andes. The Spaniards never found Machu Picchu and so, unlike other Inka cities, they never changed or destroyed it. Bingham had found a rare treasure indeed – an untouched example of the finest Inka royal architecture and stonework.

Machu Picchu drapes majestically between two peaks at the end of a perilously steep mountain ridge. Despite the challenging location, it was built with great skill and a strong sense of beauty. The stone walls seem to grow naturally from the mountain granite in perfect harmony with their lovely setting. It's a haunting place that immediately prompts questions about the people who built it. Who were these Inkas? And how did they accomplish such a difficult task? More interestingly, why?

This little Inka boy was found perfectly preserved after 500 years in the cold air at the top of one of the world's highest mountains. He was probably drugged so that he fell asleep and felt no pain as he slowly froze to death. He died knowing that he could receive no greater honor than to be chosen as an offering to the gods.

He was surrounded by precious objects. The llama wool fabric was the finest that skilled Inka weavers could produce; the small llama figurine was the work of brilliant goldsmiths. Drawstring bags contain his baby teeth and nail clippings so that he wouldn't have to search for them in the afterlife.

Understanding the Inkas is not easy. They had no written language, so they left no record of their history.

Archaeologists at work in the Andes today continue to make discoveries that tell us more about them. The more we learn, the more we wonder – can we ever really understand a culture so wildly different from our own? A culture where rocks were sacred. Where constellations were the dark spaces between the stars. Where strips of finely woven cloth were more precious than gold. Where a vast empire was expertly governed by people who had no knowledge of iron, money, the wheel, or writing. Where small, perfect children were sacrificed on frozen mountain peaks to win the favor of the gods. It's as though down were up and black were white. The Inkas are endlessly perplexing and endlessly fascinating.

In the 13th century the Inka people were a small clan of mountain dwellers, one of a hundred different tribes living in the Andes Mountains. It's not known where they came from, but they settled on a high plain where they built the town of Cuzco. In the course of two centuries the Inkas established a royal family and gradually came to dominate some of their closest neighbors. Legend says that the royal family was directly descended from the sun god, Inti, but despite their divine origin, Inka rulers didn't do anything particularly divine for many years.

Then, during the reign of the Inka ruler, Viracocha, things changed. A rival group, the Chancas, threatened the Inkas. Viracocha was terrified of the notorious Chanca warriors and fled into the mountains. His son, Pachacuti, refused to join the retreat. Inti visited him in a dream and the vision inspired him. He gathered a band of warriors and stood his ground against the Chancas. A little help from Inti at a crucial moment turned stones on the battlefield into soldiers, and the Inkas triumphed.

Pachacuti proclaimed himself the Sapa Inka (unique king) and celebrated his victory by drinking *chicha* (beer made from corn) from the hollowed-out skull of the defeated Chanca leader. It was a victory ritual that he would repeat many times as he went on to create what would become one of the largest empires the world had ever seen.

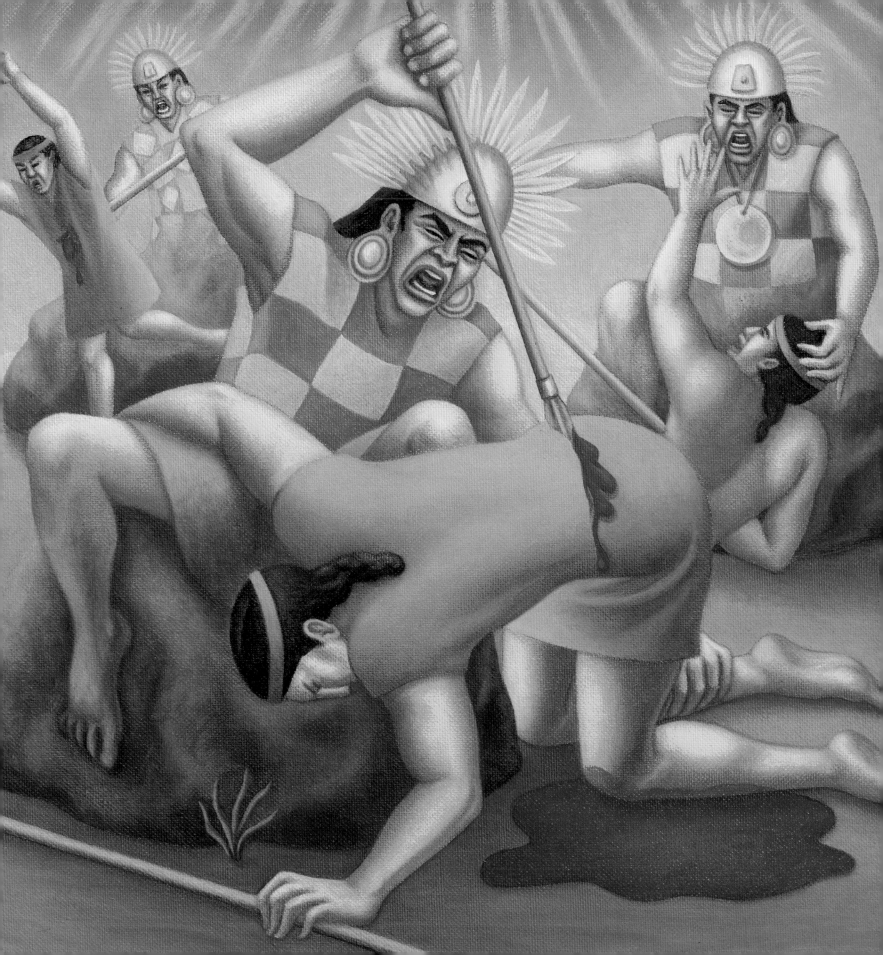

A religious ceremony. The men wore garments made of colorful bird feathers.

Men tilling the soil and women planting seeds.

The ritual sacrifice of a llama to the gods.

A warrior holding the head of an enemy.

A few Spaniards wrote down their impressions of Inka culture even as they were destroying it. They are not completely accurate, but the chronicles are the only written record of the Inkas before the Spanish. One chronicler, Felipe Guamán Poma de Ayala, accompanied his words with rough illustrations. Although he wasn't born until 50 years after the Spanish conquest, his mother was Inka and he attempted to show Inka life in his drawings.

That is the story of the beginning of the Inka Empire told from Pachacuti's point of view. It's more of a legend than an accurate history. It was intended to glorify the Inkas, and Pachacuti, and to prove the emperor's kinship with the gods. The Inkas told the story among themselves and to the people they conquered. They also told it, and many other tales, to their conquerors. The Spaniards wrote down the stories in books called chronicles, but they rewrote them from their own point of view and changed them to suit their own purposes. As a result, it's hard to know what to believe.

We can be reasonably sure that the stones on the battlefield didn't come to life to defend the Inkas. But was there really a war between the Inkas and the Chancas? Or was it an excuse invented by an ambitious son who wanted to overthrow his father? Was Pachacuti a heroic leader who led his soldiers to victory against great odds or a lucky one who happened to be in the right place at the right time? The truth will never be known.

One thing is certain, though. At some point in the 15th century the fate of the Inka people changed dramatically. Somehow they transformed themselves from a small, unremarkable group of mountain folk into mighty conquerors.

Pachacuti and his heirs eventually conquered an area so large that today all of Peru and parts of six other South American countries could be contained within its borders. Much of the territory was in the Andes, mountains so lofty that the simple act of breathing in the thin, high-altitude air was a challenge. West of the Andes, along the Pacific Ocean, the empire included one of the driest places in the world, the Atacama Desert, where not even cactus can grow. East of the Andes it included one of the wettest, the Amazon rain forest. The entire region was often battered by earthquakes and El Niño storms.

Great early civilizations have generally appeared in places (like the Nile valley in Egypt) where climate and terrain make life easier. Only in the Andes has an advanced culture been established in surroundings where life is a constant struggle for survival.

In order to communicate with distant parts of the empire, the Inkas built 15,000 miles of brilliantly engineered roads. They shaped them to fit the landscape. Wide, stone-paved avenues crossed high mountain plains, but since the Inkas didn't use wheels, their roads didn't all have to be flat and smooth. Narrow stairways climbed steep rock cliffs, and woven grass suspension bridges swayed dizzyingly above deep river valleys. To us, they hardly seem like roads, but they were all part of the Inka highway system.

Chaskis *(messengers) raced over the stones carrying messages from the emperor to his subjects. Chaskis, running in relays at top speed, could carry a message 250 miles in one day. They ate and slept in roadside rest stops called* chaski wasis *(chaski houses) while they waited for the next message.*

The Inkas called their empire Tawantinsuyo, Land of the Four Quarters. Imaginary lines radiated out from Cuzco, dividing the empire into four parts. The sky was as much a part of the Inka universe as the earth, and the heavens were similarly divided by the bright swath of stars we call the Milky Way.

Cuzco was the center of the rapidly expanding Inka world, and Pachacuti rebuilt it in keeping with its importance. He replaced its adobe huts with a stately city of stone. He covered the walls of important buildings with plates of gold and silver. In Cuzco the people who were directly descended from the original Inka tribe lived in splendor. They were the true Inkas, the nobility. They strolled in a garden whose life-size flowers, corn plants, birds, and llamas were made of gold and silver. They enjoyed exclusive privileges that were forbidden to non-Inkas. Only the nobility, for example, were allowed to wear gold and silver ear ornaments to decorate their stretched-out earlobes. It's estimated that there were 40,000 of these true Inkas living in Cuzco. From there they controlled as many as 10 million subjects.

The people that the Inkas conquered were as diverse, and as difficult, as the land they inhabited. Different tribes spoke different languages and worshiped different gods. Their customs and beliefs, their clothing, their crops, their crafts and skills all varied greatly from place to place. There was conflict, and even fighting, between them.

Often the Inkas could win the loyalty of local leaders with generous gifts of food, drink, and fine cloth, or with menacing threats, and they did so whenever they could. But if fighting was necessary, they were prepared. Large, well-trained armies of warriors marched out from Cuzco, their deadly javelins, slingshots, and war clubs at the ready.

Inka warriors sounded as fierce as they looked. They played instruments and drums and sang threatening war chants to frighten their enemies into surrendering.

Conquering the many individual, isolated tribes was probably the easy part of empire building. Governing the vast empire was far more difficult. Weaving the many different peoples into a unified nation was the real work, and the true genius, of the Inkas.

The Inkas governed according to an intricate and delicately balanced system of give and take. Using a census that was probably more accurate than any done today, they levied high taxes on every household in the empire. Because there was no such thing as money, taxes were paid with crops, textiles, and, especially, work.

Hundreds of thousands of *mit'a* laborers (people who were paying their taxes with work) served the Sapa Inka as soldiers, farmers, road builders, and settlers of new territories, doing whatever he needed. The empire could not have been built without them. They were a big part of the give and take system – the emperor gave back to them by feeding and clothing them while they worked for him. Stone *qollqas* (warehouses) throughout the empire were filled with supplies of food and cloth to be distributed to the vast armies of *mit'a* workers and presented to local leaders to ensure their loyalty to the emperor.

For the give and take to work, the Inkas had to keep careful track of thousands of details. Days of *mit'a* labor, baskets of grain, number of llamas, population, taxes paid, taxes owed, and many other things had to be accounted for without the use of written language. They devised an ingenious way of keeping records. They tied knots in fringes of colored strings called *khipus*. The type of knot, the length and color of the strings, and the positions of the knots on the strings all had meaning for those who could "read" them.

It was up to the kuraka, *the local leader, to make sure that every household in the village met the demands of the Inka tax collector.*

For the Inkas, it was not enough to conquer and tax their subjects. They wanted to control their thinking as well, so they imposed their religion on them. Conquered people were required to worship the Inka deities. Since the Sapa Inka was a god, religion and government were in many ways the same thing. By forcing their subjects to accept their religion, the Inkas were also forcing them to accept their authority as rulers. Tribes were still allowed to worship their own gods as long as the official Inka deities were supreme. The Inkas had a healthy respect for the power of the local gods and even used that power to their advantage. They took important local *wakas* (sacred objects) to Cuzco and held them hostage as a way of controlling the people who believed in them.

The Inkas were a very religious people. Their beliefs were deeply embedded in their lives. Their complicated religion was part of every day of every season and influenced everything they did. From the sun god, Inti, to Pacha Mama, mother earth, to springs and rocks and eggs with two yolks, all of nature was alive with religious meaning for the Inkas.

Inka religious beliefs were so strong that they blurred the distinction between the living and the dead. Dead Sapa Inkas were honored as if they were alive. Their mummies were offered food every day and consulted about the future when decisions had to be made.

Mountains were especially sacred. Snow-capped peaks were seen as the only dependable source of precious water in a land of scarce and unpredictable rainfall. According to Inka beliefs, melted snow flowed from mountain springs to the sacred Urubamba River and on into the ocean. From there, it rose up into the sky and flowed in the heavenly version of the Urubamba, the Milky Way, until it was time for it to return to the earth as rainfall. Because of their important place in this vital cycle, mountains were fervently worshiped.

Religion surely played a large part in Pachacuti's decision to build Machu Picchu. The landscape surrounding its site was unusually holy. The ridge was nearly encircled at its base by the Urubamba River. It was rich in natural *wakas*, such as rock formations and springs. In the distance, in all directions, many of the most sacred snow-capped mountains could be seen. It was the ideal place for Inka nobility and priests to perform the rituals, ceremonies, and sacrifices that linked them with their gods.

Machu Picchu was planned around its natural religious features. Priests and architects surveyed the terrain and noted the locations of sacred rock outcroppings and mountain peaks. They watched the movement of the sun and moon and stars past distant mountains and noticed how *wakas* lined up with the peaks during significant heavenly events, such as solstice sunrises. They took these careful observations into account when they decided where buildings would be located and in which direction windows would face.

There were also other, less spiritual reasons for building Machu Picchu. The region along the Urubamba bordered the rain forest, the only source of certain rare products that were prized by the Inkas. Coca leaves for use in religious ceremonies, brilliantly colored bird feathers for clothing and decoration, and healing jungle herbs could only be found in the rain forest. Conquering the neighboring region guaranteed that the Inkas could always get these precious goods.

Pachacuti conquered the new territory, built settlements, and connected them with a web of roads. Machu Picchu was the largest and most magnificent of all these communities. It wasn't a fortress, but the sight of it looming high above the Urubamba valley must have been intimidating to rain forest tribes who were hostile to the Inkas.

The location was difficult. Steep slopes and sheer rock cliffs plunged to the river thousands of feet below. The few small areas of level land were densely overgrown. Despite the problems it presented, the site was strategically located and breathtakingly beautiful. Most importantly, it was sacred, and Pachacuti was determined to build upon it.

Stone was the building material of choice in the Inka Empire. In a land of mud brick dwellings, the fine quality and unique style of the Inka stonework stood out. Throughout the empire, stone buildings announced the presence and the power of the Inka conquerors as nothing else could. From the palaces of Cuzco to the most remote *chaski wasi*, if it was built for Pachacuti, it was built of stone. Machu Picchu was no exception.

The ridge itself was the source of the hard gray granite used to build the city. Some stones lay loose on the ground, freed from the bedrock by earthquakes and erosion. The smallest of these field stones could be picked up and carried where they were needed. Larger ones had to be dragged.

The llamas used as pack animals in the Andes were not very strong, and they were as obstinate as they were delicate. Llamas could carry less than 100 pounds. Saddled with a heavier load they would sit down and refuse to move. *Mit'a* laborers couldn't refuse. Hundreds of them, using woven grass ropes to pull and levers to push, moved gigantic stones around the construction site. Whenever possible workers moved stones from a higher place to a lower one, letting gravity help them.

Some stones had to be quarried from the granite bedrock. They had no iron tools, so workers took advantage of natural cracks and weaknesses in the rock. They used pounding rocks and bars made of bronze (the hardest metal that the Inkas knew how to make) to force the cracks open and break the stones free.

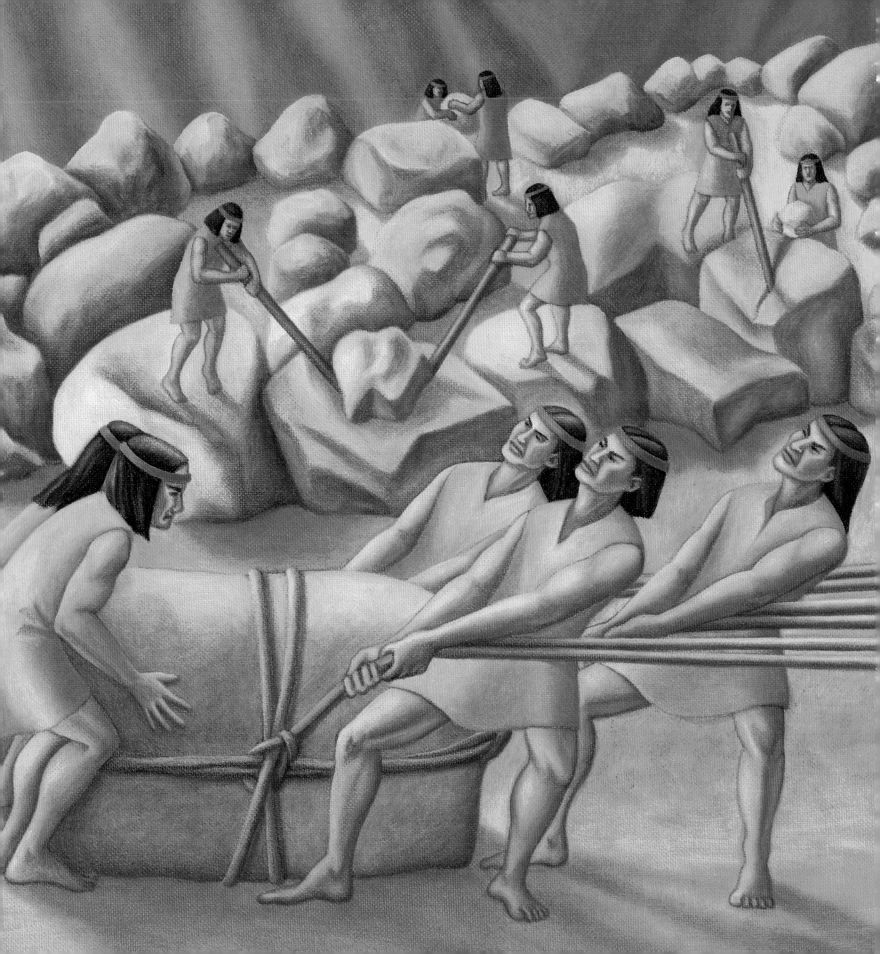

It's estimated that over 1,000 people lived in Machu Picchu. Though it wasn't an ordinary settlement, it had features that were common in other Inka towns. It was divided into a terraced agricultural area and an urban area of homes and workshops. (The urban area is above the long staircase in this painting; the agricultural area is below it.)

The urban area was divided by a series of ceremonial plazas into the *hanan* and *hurin* sectors. The *hurin* sector, to the right of the plazas, was where most people lived and worked. The *hanan* sector, to the left, was where most of the religious buildings and *wakas* were located.

An important *waka* called the Intiwatana (hitching post of the sun) was surrounded by temples at the top of a terraced hill in the *hanan* sector. Religious rituals took place on the Intiwatana hilltop and at the Sun Temple.

There were more than 3,000 steps in the staircases that linked the many levels of the steep city.

A *Intiwatana hill*
B hanan *area*
C *ceremonial plazas*
D hurin *area*
E *Sun Temple*
F *urban area*
G *agricultural area*

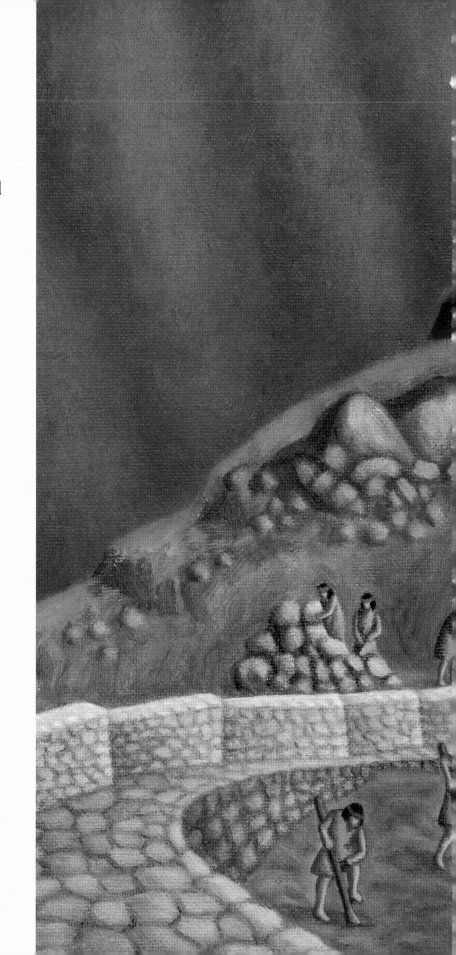

Inka stonemasons managed to do sophisticated and beautiful work with the most primitive of tools. They shaped the enormous blocks of granite using nothing more than round pounding rocks. By lifting and then dropping the pounding rocks onto the blocks, they were able to flatten each surface. Then they used smaller pounding rocks to chip precise edges. Each block had to be shaped to fit tightly against the ones already in place. Trial and error would have worked with stones small enough to be easily lifted. They could have been removed, pounded, and then replaced over and over again until the fit was right. But how was it done with boulders weighing several tons? We still don't know.

Inka stonemasons are most famous for the polygonal (many-sided) stones that they used in their most important religious buildings. While rectangular blocks have eight corners and six sides, polygonal blocks can have any number. One enormous stone embedded in a temple wall in Machu Picchu is estimated to have at least 33 corners! The difficulty of carving one polygonal block to fit snugly against another can only be imagined, but the Inkas were up to the challenge. Walls of tightly interlocked, beautifully finished polygonal stones are uniquely and characteristically Inka. Their like is seen nowhere else in the world.

It was in the important religious buildings at Machu Picchu that the most highly skilled stonemasons displayed their talents, and the Sun Temple was the finest of them all. The curved wall that encloses its natural stone *waka* is one of the most striking and beautifully made anywhere in the Inka empire.

On certain days of the year Inka nobles and priests observed the position of shadows that the rising sun cast on the *waka* through the Sun Temple windows. Many people would have traveled to Machu Picchu to be part of this ceremony. These ritualized observations of the sun not only gave the Inkas a spiritual connection with Inti, they provided vital practical information as well, such as when to prepare the soil for planting.

It was never intended that the agricultural terraces of Machu Picchu would provide enough food for all the residents. Since it was a religious sanctuary, much of the corn grown there would probably have been used to brew ceremonial *chicha* or burned as offerings to the gods.

But residents hardly went hungry. Many of the nobles who lived at Machu Picchu were members of Pachacuti's *panaka,* his extended family. Naturally Pachacuti made sure that they had everything they needed. Herds of llamas and trains of heavily laden porters traveled the roads to Machu Picchu carrying food from nearby farming communities and luxury items from the jungle and from Cuzco.

Since one of the important responsibilities of the *panaka* was to care for the emperor's mummy, the porters would have continued to bring supplies after Pachacuti's death.

The *panaka* members lived in comfort in Machu Picchu. Exotic fruits and herbs and animals were always available from the nearby jungle valley, but because the city was thousands of feet higher, the climate was cool enough for mountain dwellers. Thanks to the tremendous wealth of the Inka Empire, life was easy and luxurious. Work was done, of course. Terraces were planted and crops were harvested. The emperor's chosen women, the *aclla*, wove beautifully patterned cloth and brewed *chicha*. Stonemasons were always at work on new building.

It was a special place. Its residents had every reason to believe that their protected, holy existence would last forever.

In fact, it hardly lasted a century.

The end came abruptly and brutally. Spanish explorers arrived in Central America at the end of the 1400s, bringing with them smallpox and other European diseases. The diseases were deadly to New World people who had never been exposed to them and whose bodies had no immunity to them. An epidemic swept southward, spreading rapidly from tribe to tribe, killing millions of people. The diseases reached the Andes long before the Spaniards themselves did. It's estimated that two-thirds of the Andean population died during this time.

In 1528, the Inka emperor Wayna Capac died, probably of smallpox, and so did the son he had chosen to be his successor. Two other sons, Atawalpa, who lived in the northern part of the empire, and Wascar in Cuzco in the south, both claimed the right to be emperor. Their rivalry plunged all of Tawantinsuyo into a bloody civil war. The empire was already weakened because so many people, Inkas and Inka subjects alike, had died of disease. The war caused even more destruction.

Atawalpa sent soldiers to Cuzco to attack his half-brother's armies. They captured Wascar and the civil war was over. Atawalpa had won. He was free to move back to Cuzco and take his rightful position as emperor.

During the long walk south to Cuzco, strangers approached Atawalpa's camp. They were odd-looking creatures, not at all like people from the Andes. Their clothing was peculiar, and they had hair on their faces. They sat atop powerful animals that were larger than the largest llama. The strangers requested a meeting between their leader and the emperor in the nearby town of Cajamarca. They seemed friendly, and they numbered fewer than 200 altogether. Surely they were not a threat. Atawalpa agreed to the meeting. The next day, he and his retinue of thousands set off at a leisurely pace. Dressed in fine, colorful clothes, chanting and playing musical instruments, their slow approach to Cajamarca hardly seemed like a march to a fate that would ultimately shatter their world.

Francisco Pizarro, leader of the Spaniards, had laid a trap in Cajamarca. He and his soldiers sat hunched on their horses inside the low buildings surrounding the town square. They were professional soldiers, famous for their bravery, but they knew they were horribly outnumbered. They were frightened, and waiting only increased their terror.

Atawalpa arrived at last in the late afternoon, and his followers passed through the narrow gate and crowded into the empty square. A Catholic priest stepped forward to meet him. Through an interpreter, the priest attempted to convert the Sapa Inka to Christianity. Atawalpa, angry at the insult to the Inka gods, refused the foreign religion and knocked the priest's Bible to the ground.

This was the chance that Pizarro needed. He had been bound by orders from his church forbidding him to harm New World people unless they rejected Christianity. When Atawalpa struck the Bible, Pizarro leaped into action. He gave a signal and two cannons fired into the crowd. His soldiers spurred their horses and burst out into the square, steel swords slashing. Surprised, unarmed, trapped, paralyzed with fear at the booming cannonfire and the sight of steel-helmeted men towering above them on horseback, Atawalpa's men panicked. The slaughter began. Two hours later, Atawalpa was a prisoner and 7,000 of his people lay dead.

With the emperor as their hostage, the conquerors could easily control a nation already crippled by disease and civil war. Atawalpa wanted only to free himself from his captors. He had noticed the Spanish hunger for precious metals and thought he could turn their greed to his advantage. He suggested a ransom. Placing his hand on the wall above his head, he offered to fill the room to that height, once with gold and twice with silver, in exchange for his life. Pizarro was quick to agree.

Inka subjects, following Atawalpa's orders, and Pizarro's soldiers, following his, ransacked every city and stripped every temple from Cajamarca to Cuzco and beyond. Furnaces blazed night and day, melting beautifully crafted statues, wall decorations, cups, and jewelry down into lumps of metal. Thousands of pounds of gold and silver were shipped to Spain. Despite the fantastic ransom, Pizarro didn't release Atawalpa. He killed him.

They were very thorough, but somehow no one, Inkas, Inka subjects, or Spaniards, ever searched Machu Picchu. How could this have been? How could such an important place have been overlooked?

We'll never know exactly what happened, but apparently the changes in the Andean world had already affected Machu Picchu before the Spaniards arrived. It's possible that, during the confusion of the civil war, supplies were no longer sent to Pachacuti's *panaka*, leaving the residents without food. It's also possible that the epidemic was particularly deadly there. Whatever the reason, Machu Picchu was abandoned before the Spanish arrived in the Andes. Everything of value was removed, and the buildings were left to the engulfing jungle. It disappeared from memory.

The residents of Machu Picchu left behind little more than the stones of their buildings, but for Hiram Bingham and the archaeologists who came after him, it has been a treasure trove. Studying other Inka towns has been like trying to read a book whose pages have been torn out. In Machu Picchu the pages of the book are blurred by time, but at least they are still there.

Other scholars have joined archaeologists in studying Machu Picchu, with their own approaches to learning about the Inkas. Architects examine the design of the buildings, and astronomers ponder the skies above the city. Stonemasons and sculptors puzzle over the remarkable stonework. Anthropologists talk with modern descendants of the Inkas in the area, looking for clues to what life might have been like 500 years earlier.

Today visitors to Machu Picchu gather at sunrise to watch as the sky grows light. The air warms and mist billows up from the Urubamba valley far below. Birdsong suddenly fills the air. In the distance, in every direction, the embracing mountain peaks are dark against the pale sky. The moment is beautiful, magical beyond belief. Though we are a long way from understanding the Inkas, Machu Picchu allows us a glimpse of the world as they saw it.

Glossary

aclla–*women chosen to serve the Sapa Inka because of their special skills in weaving and brewing chicha and because of their beauty*

chaski–*swift foot messenger*

chaski wasi–*building by the side of the road used by the chaskis*

chicha–*beer made from corn and used in religious ceremonies*

hanan–*area of an Inka town where important religious buildings and wakas were located*

hurin–*area of an Inka town where homes and workshops were located*

Inka–*Originally the word Inka referred only to the ruler (the Sapa Inka, or unique king). It also referred to the nobility, the people who were the descendants of the original Inka people. Nowadays it refers to anyone who lived under Inka rule, whether they were direct Inka descendants or conquered Inka subjects. It also refers to the time of Inka rule and its style of art.*

Inti–*the Inka sun god*

khipu–*a device for keeping records using strings and knots*

kuraka–*a local tribal leader*

mit'a–*work done as a duty to the Sapa Inka*

panaka–*extended family of the Sapa Inka*

qollqa–*storehouse*

Sapa Inka–*unique king, the emperor*

Tawantinsuyo–*Inka name for their empire, meaning Land of the Four Quarters*

waka–*a sacred religious object, either natural or humanmade*

Author's note: There is more than one way to spell many Inka words. Inka, for example, is often Inca. As there was no written form of the Inka language in the 16th century, the Spanish chroniclers wrote down the sounds they heard according to the way Spanish was written. Today native speakers in the Andes are moving away from the spellings of the conquerors. Among other things, "k" has replaced the Spanish "c." These spellings are respected by most scholars whose work is the study of Inka culture. These are the spellings I've chosen to use in this book.

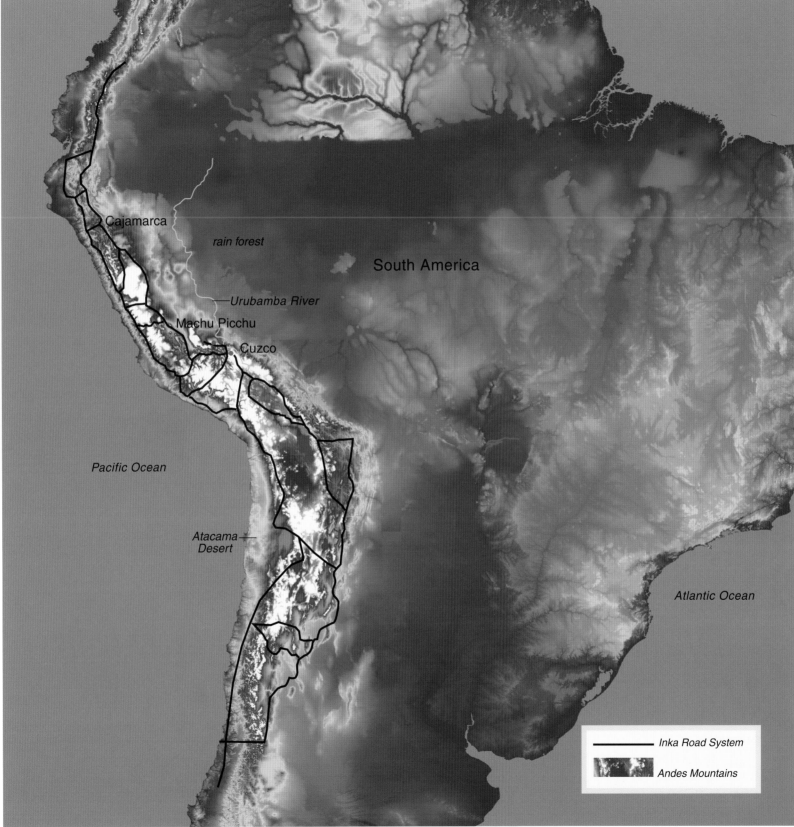

Cajamarca

rain forest

South America

—Urubamba River

Machu Picchu

Cuzco

Pacific Ocean

Atacama Desert

Atlantic Ocean

Inka Road System

Andes Mountains

Index

Aclla, 36

Amazon rain forest, 12, 23

Andes Mountains, 4, 8, 12, 20, 24, 39-40, 43

Archaeologists, 7, 45

Atacama Desert, 12

Atawalpa, 39-40, 43

Bingham, Hiram, 4, 45

Cajamarca, 40, 43

Chancas, 8, 11

Chaskis, 12, 24

Chicha, 8, 35-36

Chronicles, Spanish, 10, 11

Cuzco, 8, 15, 19, 24, 35, 39-40, 43

El Niño, 12

Gold, 6, 15, 43

Government, 16, 19

Hanan, 27

Hurin, 27

Inka Empire, 8, 11, 15-16, 24, 32, 36, 39

Inti, 9, 19, 32

Intihuatana, 27

Khipus, 16

Kuraka, 16

Llamas, 16, 24, 35, 40

Milky Way, 15, 20

Mit'a labor, 16, 24

Mummy, 6, 19, 35

Nobility, 15, 20, 35

Pachacuti, 4, 8, 11-12, 15, 20, 23-24, 35, 43

Pacha Mama, 19

Panaka, 35-36, 43

Pizarro, Francisco, 40, 43

Poma de Ayala, Felipe Guaman, 10

Qollqas, 16

Religion, 19-20, 32, 35

Roads, 12

Sapa Inka, 8, 16, 19, 40

Smallpox, 39

Spaniards, 4, 10-11, 39-40, 43, 45

Stonework, 4, 24, 26, 32, 36, 45

Sun Temple, 27, 32

Tawantinsuyu, 15, 39

Taxes, 16, 19

Terraces, agricultural, 27, 35-36

Urubamba River, 4, 20, 23, 45

Viracocha, 8

Wacas, 19-20, 27, 32, 45

Warriors, 10, 15, 39-40

Wascar, 39

Wayna Capac, 39

Weaving, 6, 36

Credits

Amy Crehore: pp. *5, 9, 13, 14, 17, 18 , 21, 22, 25, 27, 28-31, 33, 34, 37, 38, 41,42*

Elizabeth Mann: *pp. 44-45*

Loren McIntyre/ National Geographic Image Collection: *p. 6*

Nick Saunders/ Barbara Heller Photo Library, London/ Art Resource, NY: *p. 10*